The Little Black Book of Out of the Box Investments

Winning Strategies to Grow Your Investments

[:Copyright:] © 2019 by Boris Timm - amazon.com/author/boris-timm

All rights reserved. No part of this publication may be reproduced, distributed, or transmitted in any form or by any means, including photocopying, recording, or other electronic or mechanical methods, without the prior written permission of the publisher, except in the case of brief quotations embodied in critical reviews and certain other noncommercial uses permitted by copyright law.

Although every precaution has been taken to verify the accuracy of the information contained herein, the author and publisher assume no responsibility for any errors or omissions. No liability is assumed for damages that may result from the use of information contained within.

Table of Contents

Introduction 1

Chapter 1
   Strategy Overview 3
      What Does Strategy Mean to You? 4
      What Comes First - Finance Strategy or
      Business Strategy? 7

Chapter 2
   Build Your Investment Strategy to Meet
   Your Goals 12

Chapter 3
   Managed Funds: Growing Your Wealth without the
   Headaches 16

Chapter 4
   Unlimited Winning Strategies on How to Grow
   Your Wealth 21

Chapter 5
   Winning Strategy for Using Social
   Media to Grow Your Wealth 34

Chapter 6
   What Marketing Strategy is the Best
   for You to Grow Your Wealth? 38

Chapter 7
   Financial Asset Management - Manage Your
   Wealth 45
      6 Questions to Test Your Wealth Building
      Strategies 47
      Why is Wealth Management Important? 51

Chapter 8
   Avoiding Financial Disaster in Wealth Building .. 54

Chapter 9
    The Most Important Rule of Investing to Build Your Wealth 64

Chapter 10
    The Fundamental Secret of Wealth 67

Chapter 11
    Wealth Management and Wealth Attraction 69

Chapter 12
    Applying SWOT (Strengths, Weaknesses, Opportunities, and Threats) Analysis to Growing Wealth 73

Chapter 13
    The Dangers in Wealth Building 79

Conclusion 84

Introduction

People will always stress that having a well researched business plan is key before you start your business. Although creating a business plan is often an important step in the evolution of a business, particularly if you need financing or you are not experienced at running a business, it is not necessarily the essential first step.

According to the Collins English Dictionary, strategy is "a particular long-term plan for success". For our purposes, we will consider the essence of strategy as a formula for coping with the competition.

Competitive strategy is about being different and the goal for a corporate strategy is to find a position in the industry where the company is unique and can defend itself against market forces. To do this the company must choose a set of activities that can deliver a unique mix of value.

There are two key elements that should be completed prior to the business plan: the business model and the strategy

While the word model often stirs up images of mathematical formulas, a business model is in fact a story of how a business works. In general terms, a business model is the method of doing business by which a company can generate revenue.

Both start-up ventures and established companies take new products and services to the market through a venture shaped by a specific business model. In their paper, The Role of the Business Model in Capturing Value from Innovation.

The determination of a strategy is rooted in determining how a company stacks up against basic market forces, how it can defend itself against these forces and how it can influence these forces.

The focus of this eBook is present the winning strategies to grow your wealth. This will be done in line with your business in view.

However I wouldn't want to take it for granted that the word strategy is clearly understood by all and sundry. Therefore let me clarify the term strategy in chapter one.

Chapter 1

Strategy Overview

According to the Collins English Dictionary, strategy is "a particular long-term plan for success". For our purposes, we will consider the essence of strategy as a formula for coping with the competition.

Competitive strategy is about being different and the goal for a corporate strategy is to find a position in the industry where the company is unique and can defend itself against market forces. To do this the company must choose a set of activities that can deliver a unique mix of value.

Strategy is a well-thought through and succinct plan of where you want your business to be in 5 years' time and what resources that you do not have now you will put in place to get there. It is also fluid and will never remain static.

Be prepared for and accept the fact that your strategic plan must evolve regularly as circumstances change and new opportunities present themselves.

Of course that is an over-simplification of a long process that leads to the succinct plan. You absolutely do have to answer the following:

What is my product or service?

Who are my competitors and how do they do business?

Who are my clients going to be and how am I going to reach them?

What is the total market for my product or service and how much of it do I want?

What does a SWOT analysis tell me?

How am I going to make a profitable return (and, on this, remember that turnover is bling but cash is king!)

There are many other strategic tools to use and you can be as complicated in your analysis as you want. But if you don't have a clear, succinct and adaptable plan at the end of it you have wasted your time.

What Does Strategy Mean to You?

Most effective strategy processes begin with a stock-take: a review and assessment of the organization's current products, markets and customers. This is an essential first step to kicking off a good strategy-setting exercise.

Yet no strategy process that I have come across conducts an even more crucial preliminary activity - even before the one described above. This is to ask what the sponsor of the strategy process thinks of when he or she thinks about strategy. What, in effect, does strategy mean to you?

Everyone leading or facilitating a strategy review should ask this question. The answers may amaze you. And they may make the sponsor quite uncomfortable.

The reason is that most people in business have a very different idea of what strategy really means. Unless a facilitator unpacks the organization's perception about what a strategy means to them, then success is unlikely. It becomes impossible to determine what must be delivered.

For some executives, a strategy will be the way they hope to increase the share price over the next year. For others, it will mean sorting out which take-over candidates it should approach.

One of my clients saw strategy as determining how to negotiate a management buy-out from the majority shareholder. Still others will see strategy in a purer light: what is the long term future that we can envision for the company, and what is the best route to get there?

None of these different perceptions of strategy is wrong. They are the sponsor's genuinely held beliefs. But each represents a starting point in the sponsor's mind about why a strategy was seen to be required. And a facilitator of strategy needs to understand these at the start.

But there's even more to it than this.

As well as understanding what has precipitated the need for strategy, we need to unpick what the sponsor sees as its essential components. Is its emphasis a vision, and if so what is the timescale?

Is the focus more towards medium or short-term action - more of a tactical plan in fact? Does it need to focus more on people and the internal culture? Or is the driving issue to do with fast-changing markets?

One organization I worked with realized after the strategy was complete that the real objective was to educate the Board and executive team.

The unspoken secret in all strategy-setting exercises is that strategy means different things to different people. Each different understanding of strategy is valid, because each organization and its strategy team are different. But these different views of strategy mean that quite radically different approaches to strategy development need to be taken.

What Comes First - Finance Strategy or Business Strategy?

Everyone knows business strategy and finance strategy are interrelated. But which one should dictate?

If you are an entrepreneur, your future is your most valuable asset. Let's face it- investors can only generate interest on their money. It takes an entrepreneur to generate profit!

For an entrepreneur, business strategy must dictate finance - never the reverse. Everyone knows business strategy and finance strategy are interrelated. But which one should dictate?

The first place to start is to imagine the future you would want if you had unlimited resources.

When Wayne got turned down by the bank for the $1 million he needed to grow is business, he made an assumption that resources were scare and expensive. Wayne began to dwarf his vision of his company's future.

That's what happens when you let finance strategy dictate business strategy. Wayne was not even aware of the assumption he had made or the devastating effect on his company- until I brought this to his attention.

We worked with Wayne to re-vision his potential, assuming unlimited resources, built upon his deep and real passion and developed a strategy that resulted in him attracting $10m for a minority stake of his company.

How did an entrepreneur who got turned down by the bank for $1 million get $10 million and keep control? Certainly not based on his past!! He shared his passion about the future he really wanted to build!

When you follow your passion you get the best outcomes: You easily attract customers, vendors, talent and finance. Pursuing your passion lets you capture your best opportunities- for profitable growth. Faster. Safer.

When you don't follow your passion, you end up with a sub-optimal strategy. The result is extra risk making it much harder to attract customers, vendors, talent and especially financing.

When you follow your passion and harness it with a powerful, directed business strategy, better financing results. This is the right way to link passion and key strategic thinking and implementation to achieve your Optimum Growth Strategy.

Effective Strategies in Business

During what many refer to as a period of global recession the challenges of work/life balance and leveraging time, money and energy are even more pertinent now than ever before.

Proper resourcing and effective strategy are even more essential. For example it is essential in your business armoury to be surrounded by resources that enable you to explore proper funding for your business along with expert advice to maintain business growth or turnaround strategies should things start to go pear shaped.

If the most successful in business have experienced bankruptcy on the way to success you and I are no less immune to that event.

Individual competition is not the only way forward. The value of working collaboratively in such things as joint ventures can prove more lucrative than individual effort alone when done in a meaningful way.

Whether we like it or not internet technology has significantly impacted the way people do business and if you do not have an online presence with an internet marketing strategy your business is in danger of falling apart.

It is a bit like the day when you could still buy cassettes and now DVDs are the new media.

However many are still intimidated by the internet world and the learning curve that goes with it.

In response to the many challenges one of the things at Business Giants Network that we attempt to redress through membership is the balance between proper resourcing and effective strategy and marketing under one roof.

The fact that Business Giants Network pays their network owners is not so much a recession solution but more of a value statement on our part for their time and commitment to building a community where people can do more business.

An example of effective strategy is that currently at network meetings your audience are those directly in front of you.

What we are providing through membership is the opportunity of live recording and through the use of Business Giants Network marketing platform your educational slot now goes out to the rest of the world. Now your ten minute slot has greater educational and marketing power.

You can see from this example how online marketing can leverage your offline activities.

Internet and offline marketing does not have to feel so intimidating when you partner with those that have that expertise.

A funding consultancy and a business rescue service as well as a family success support centre have also arisen in response to the business challenges cited.

You can see further examples on the video series on my site but in the meantime take an audit of what you have in place to address resourcing, strategy and marketing, identify any gaps and set about a plan to bridge those gaps in order to strengthen the platform on which you do business.

Chapter 2

Build Your Investment Strategy to Meet Your Goals

Establishing an investment strategy that meets your personality and your goals is relatively easy once you determine whether you want a conservative investment strategy or a moderate investment strategy. This requires two primary actions.

First, Establish Your Personality and Goals

What kind of risk are you willing to accept? A few losses will always occur but are you willing to accept only minor losses or do you want to shoot for large gains that may results in more losses in the process?

How often do you want to trade? Are you willing to trade each week or would you prefer only once or twice a month or even less?

Are you willing to see your portfolio, your retirement account, or wealth account build very gradually over time or do you want to grow these fast?

Second, understand the strategy ingredients that make for conservative investments and moderate or aggressive investments:

Frequent trading, almost daily, is best suited for aggressive and in some cases moderate investments.

Setting sell stops that are low, like 1% to 3% will results in more frequent trading than sell stops that are a bit higher.

Trading a wide range of stocks versus ETFs or many mutual funds will generally produce more aggressive or moderate investment strategies.

Setting different rules or parameters in your retirement software or personal investments software can affect your results and define your investment strategy as either conservative, moderate or aggressive:

a) Ranking - setting sell rules based on the rank of a position (ticker symbol) in you group of potential positions. Ranking in the top 5% or 10% vs. the top 30% will produce more frequent trading and normally a more aggressive strategy.

b) Stops - setting the sell rules based on how much a position drops from its high point can also result in trading frequency, churning of your portfolio.

c) Hold rules - defining your strategy by saying you prefer to hold positions for no less than 10 days vs. 30 or 60 days sets up your strategy for aggressive vs. conservative.

d) Employing a Market Exit signal based on the equity curve of the performance of the stock markets can tell you when to pause or even cash out of the markets for a short or long time and by doing so preserve your money from losses.

But setting this signal with a short evaluation period versus a long period can have a major effect: too long being bad because you won't get a signal in time to avert major loss, but to short will have you again trading too frequently.

e) Period of Analysis - when you are analyzing your group of potential funds, ETFs or stocks the time period selected will also determine the type of investment strategy. Longer analysis periods will result in more conservative approaches while short periods, like 10 days, will be more aggressive and require more trading.

All these factors are not as intimidating as they may sound. The key to safe investing, to defining your investment strategy, is to understand that you are in control and that you can set these parameters to meet your personality and your objectives.

Yes, you should back test to find the exact settings that meet your needs and reflect your desires in your investment software, but you can tailor the analysis testing to fall within your range of what is acceptable to you.

Chapter 3

Managed Funds: Growing Your Wealth without the Headaches

Managed funds are an easy way to invest wisely and with low risk. Investment in a fixed term deposit - especially with a fund that invests in real estate - is an easy way to grow to your wealth.

Apart from being a great way to have your money managed by investment professionals, managed funds also simplify the process of building and maintaining an investment portfolio. Instead of tracking a wide range of individual investments, your fund will keep track for you, and the progress of your investment is expressed in one simple unit price.

With any investment strategy diversification is important to minimise risk. The resources available to financial institutions are usually greater than those of the individual investor, therefore diversification is much easier as part of a managed fund than it would be if you had to raise the capital for a truly diverse - and therefore more secure - investment yourself.

As an example, if you have $100,000 to invest and you choose to buy real estate, your $100,000 might buy you a small unit that you could rent out. Then your entire financial future hangs on the performance of this one investment.

If houses in that area depreciate due to changes in the locale, or you have trouble finding or keeping tenants, or you find out three weeks too late that there are serious structural problems, your financial future is in jeopardy.

By comparison, a managed fund that invests in mortgages has the capital to speculate on a wide range of properties in diverse suburbs, with differing land values, various land uses (residential, commercial etc), and a much lower dependence on the performance of any single investment property.

Your future no longer hinges on one little unit because it's merely a part of a much larger portfolio than you could invest in on your own.

Choosing a Managed Fund

When you're choosing a managed fund it's always tempting to just go with the one that offers the best term deposit rate. However, experience dictates that it's wiser to conduct some deeper research before committing yourself to a fund. Here are some issues to consider:

The decision-makers: What qualifications do the Directors of the fund have? How closely are they involved in the day-to-day running and major investment decisions of the fund?

Any managed fund that you invest in should be run by industry professionals - accountants, brokers, people with backgrounds in banking and finance; if you're investing in a managed fund that invests heavily in property, the decision-making team should include someone with extensive experience in the real estate market.

Mortgage funds - choosing properties and quality mortgages: Mortgages are very popular investments for managed funds. As mentioned above, any fund that invests in property should have ready access to advice from a real estate market professional.

Consider factors such as the diversification of the properties invested in (geographical diversification - are the properties spread throughout a wide range of suburbs and price brackets?

And sector diversification - what property types are invested in, spread across residential, commercial, industrial etc); and what percentage of the value of the property the fund will lend (often 70% of the value for first mortgages, and up to 85% of the value of the property for second mortgages).

A good way to gauge the viability of a managed mortgage fund is to look at the number of loan write-offs; the number of bad debts incurred (mortgages that the fund has granted that have been defaulted on); and the amount of loans in arrears of principal and interest for over 30 days.

Also, every property that is invested in should be valued by a qualified valuer - not a real estate 'market appraisal' - and, if possible (especially for smaller funds), every proposed property should be inspected by a qualified employee from your fund to double check that everything is as it should be - good quality control can prevent mishaps.

Income options: Naturally, it's your choice how long you wish to invest your money for. When choosing a fund look at factors such as early withdrawal penalties and payment options.

Can you have access to the interest earned monthly? Quarterly? Annually? Or will you have to wait until the end of your fixed term period before earning any income from your investment? Choose whichever option suits you best.

A high rate of return is useless if you envisage needing an income from your investment before the end of the proposed fixed term.

Environment: Economic trends and possible political changes are some other factors to keep a weather eye out for. If you invest heavily in a fund that in turn invests internationally, you'll want to know where your money is going and whether the governments and economies in question are stable and likely to stay that way.

Some financial advisors suggest that investing 15-20% of your capital overseas is a wise move, and it is - as long as the country/countries in question have a good economic climate and aren't in the throws of political upheavals.

So, now you have a few tips for finding yourself a managed fund that will help to grow your wealth. Once you've chosen a fund, or have decided on the sorts of investments that you'd like to be involved with and you're looking for a fund, there are still some more things to consider before diving in.

Chapter 4

Unlimited Winning Strategies on How to Grow Your Wealth

Step 1: Focus on Your Goals

What are your goals for investing? It's important that you know what your main goal is before you decide what you will invest in. It's important to know your timeline. If you're investing for immediate income, than tax liens would not be a good investment vehicle for you.

Some investments are short term and some take longer to produce the desired result. How much profit do you want and how much risk are you willing to take? Higher profit usually comes with a higher risk. What I love about tax lien investing is that you can get higher profit without extremely high risk.

Do you need to keep your investments liquid, which might be the case if you are retiring soon, or have some short terms goals that you need to meet? Get clear on what your goal is for investing and then you can choose an investment vehicle that fits your goal.

Step 2: Map out Your Investment Strategy

Once you know what your goal is and you've decided on your investment vehicle, then it's helpful to map out a strategy. What exactly will you invest in? Where will you invest? How often will you need to add to your investment?

With tax lien investing for example you may want to pick a state to invest in. Most states will have tax sales at one time of the year, so you can plan how much money you will invest and when you will be investing.

Then, depending on which state you invest in, you may also need to plan on when you will be paying the subsequent taxes which will be added to your lien(s). You'll also know when the redemption period will end and when you're likely to be paid on your liens and can reinvest your profits.

Step 3: Stick With One Strategy Until You See Results

Ok, so you've started investing, and you may even have spent some money getting educated as to how to make money using a certain investment strategy.

But now you've just heard about another investment that sounds even better than the one that you're doing, so you drop everything midstream and buy another program to learn another investment strategy that supposed to make you rich.

If you keep jumping ship to try the next newest get rich quick scheme, you'll never finish anything that you start, in which case you'll never make any money. Stick with one thing until you see results, then if the results aren't what you expected, then you can look elsewhere.

But don't expect miracles, remember, if something sounds too good to be true it probably is. Look for investments with realistic - not pie in the sky results. If you're satisfied with the profit from your investment, then you'll want to go on to step 4

Step 4: Reinvest Your Profits

When I had tax liens redeem there was always something to spend the money on, bills, college tuition for one of my kids, or taxes to pay on real estate. But for your money to grow, you need to reinvest your profit.

Spend the capital investment if you need to, but take your profit and reinvest it as soon as you have the opportunity. One way that I finally started doing this was to invest through a self directed IRA instead of with after tax money.

I still do some investing outside of my self-directed IRA but at least half of my investing is through my retirement account. That way I know that when tax liens redeem all the money will be re-invested and I won't be tempted to use it.

So how do you know whether you should invest with IRA money or after tax money? That's where step 5 comes in.

Step 5: Strategize With Your Accountant to Maximize Your Tax Situation

Don't wait until tax time to sit down with your accountant or CPA. I usually like to talk to my accountant before the end of each year and have a strategy session to see where I'll stand come tax time.

There are things that you can still do even after the year is over to minimize your taxes or maximize your tax return - like contributing to your self-directed IRA. You can contribute to your retirement account through the date you file your tax return and have it apply to the previous year to lower your income and the amount of taxes you have to pay.

But some things have to be done by the end of the year. For instance if you know that you're going to owe a lot of taxes, you might want to pay outstanding bills and make tax deductible purchases before the end of the year rather than wait until the new year.

Or, if you know you are going to have a bigger tax dept next year you might want to wait and spend the money after the first of the year. Find a good accountant that can help you make the most of all the legal ways to minimize your tax dept.

Step 6: Protect Your Assets with a Trust

For this step you will need to talk to a good asset protection lawyer and it will cost you some money to open a trust account and have your assets transferred to a trust that will protect you from a law suit or judgment.

You never know what can happen in the future and it's better to be protected than to be open to have everything that you have worked for taken away from you.

Also if anything happens to you, you won't have to worry about your loved ones. Your trust will live on and your assets will be transferred to your beneficiaries without having to pay inheritance taxes.

There is a reason why the wealthy have trusts. I am not an expert in this at all, but I can recommend an attorney who is. Tim Berry is an attorney who specializes in asset protection.

Step 7. Stockpiling: Using Down to Go Up

"Stockpiling" is a term used by Phil Town in his New York Time #1 Bestseller, "Payback Time". Stockpiling is a somewhat counter-intuitive, upside-down stock investing strategy - you buy stock in businesses you love, and then hope the price will go down even further so you can buy some more.

Sounds strange at first but the key here is simply to make sure the value of the stock is substantially greater than the price you are paying for it. The more the price goes down, the better it is for you as the average cost of your investment per share goes down.

The one and only secret to stockpiling is to make sure the value of the business is substantially greater than the price you are paying for it. The key word here is value. You need to understand how to value a stock (using EPS, P/E Ratio, Minimum Acceptable Rate of Return etc.,) and give yourself a decent Margin of Safety.

The spirit of "stockpiling" is to only buy stocks in a business you'd be excited to own all of (if you could J). Then you hope the price goes down so you can "stash" as much as you can afford at as low a price as possible. Beautiful!

Step 8. Cash is Trash, Get Some Metal

Nowadays people prefer gold in their hands to cash in the bank and who could blame 'em! Hedging against inflation with gold is a time-tested strategy used by investors. That said, you don't need to buy bars of gold and bury them in your back yard (just yet!).

However, everyone should have some gold and silver in their investment portfolio. Even as little as 10%. Why? Because the real value of cash is in rapid decline - inflation and a global banking crisis means you really can't afford to leave large dollops of cash residing in savings accounts.

Also, currencies like the Euro and Dollar are on shaky ground. We're in the midst of a global currency war if you ask me. Even the Swiss Franc, traditionally a global safe haven for traders, isn't a great hedge right now, as recently the Swiss National Bank in an effort to protect their just set a ceiling on the value of the currency (first time since 1978).

So, gold and silver become apparent safe havens for anxious investors. Although knocking around the $1, 600-$1,800/ounce ceiling of late, Gold is predicted by some quarters to rise higher even as far as $2,500/ounce before the end of the year!

If you don't feel comfortable buying gold bullion in the form of bars or gold coins, then you can simply buy the SPDR Gold Trust ETF (Tracker Symbol: GLD), the world's biggest Exchange Traded Fund tracking the price of gold.

Silver, which had been on an upward trend since May 2011 and hovering around $41-$43/ounce, has corrected recently to around $30/ounce. Gold (and silver) are in the midst of a massive sell off as investors try to cover losses in other asset classes.

The price of Silver is often tied to the price of gold but Silver is the most volatile of all the precious metals. So be careful. When market sentiment eventually shifts regarding gold (and it will!) values can slide in the other direction faster than an ice cube down your back.

For those of you with an iPhone I recommend you download the Gold Price app otherwise check out their website (goldprice.org) for latest price and news on Silver and Gold.

Step 9. Savers are Losers: Repurpose Your Savings

I think hoarding your cash in a savings account for 2 or 3 years is a stupid idea and why savers become losers. Saving cash is a stupid long-term strategy but a smart short-term tactic. Let me explain...

I'm a huge fan of saving as a key habit and tactic in building your wealth. Even if you're a multi-millionaire already but you're not saving at least 10% of your gross (or net) income; you are going to get your financial ass kicked if you haven't developed the discipline and financial understanding behind saving.

Saving is the #1 financial habit to develop. Start with 10% of your gross, push this to net 10% if you can. The important thing about saving cash is to not let it sit in low-yielding bank savings account for more than 6-9 months. You can't hide in cash. You need to repurpose those savings into investments quickly. Why? Well, if you compare your net saving yields against average inflation rates you usually never make a dime!

Check out Dr. John Demartini's FAST (Forced Accelerated Savings Techniques)- he proposes you increase your savings automatically by 10% each quarter! I'm a big fan of Demartini's mindset and approach to money management and wealth building.

What I like about this method is that it forces you to focus on your net cash flow (Net Income after Taxes and Living Expenses). So, you've either got to find ways of reducing your effective tax rate or increase your gross income...or both!!

Bonus Step 10: Take Care of Your Body and Spirit

"What good will it for a man if he gains the whole world but forfeits his sole? Or what can a man give in exchange for his sole" - Matt 16:26

Sometimes we are so busy trying to make ends meet or trying to get ahead and be successful that we forget why we are doing it. All the money in the world did not help Steve Jobs when he died of cancer.

Fortunately for Mr. Jobs, he enjoyed an accomplished life in which he contributed much to society and was able to enrich is own life and that of his family. But what about you, will you work hard to amass enough money to retire comfortably only to find out that you will not be around to enjoy it? What are you doing for your health?

And what about your spiritual welfare? What will become of your soul when you leave this world and go to the next? Have you spent any time thinking about why you are here, what your true purpose is in this life and what awaits you in the next?

What a shame it would be to have all the wealth you want now and then leave it all behind with nothing to show for it. To have done nothing to lift your fellow man, or to have made this world a better place.

Step 11. Winning Strategies for Working from Home Successfully

Having a home-based business is a great option for many people. The benefits of working from home are fantastic--no commute, you can work in your pajamas, you can spend more time with your family, and the list goes on! Interestingly, some of the benefits are drawbacks as well.

When you work in the same place you live, your work and everyday lives are often hard to separate. Working from home successfully takes organization and planning. Here are some tips for working from home successfully.

Have a plan. Each morning I outline what needs to be done during the day. For me, this might include laundry, playdates, volunteer commitments, etc. as well as business tasks. Then I give myself a time-frame for each task that needs to be accomplished.

Sure things come up and I have to adjust. But knowing what needs to be accomplished that day helps me know how to shuffle things around when I need to.

Get rid of "time-suckers." You know what I'm talking about--TV, surfing the internet without a purpose, checking your e-mail 900 times a day, etc. We even went so far as to cut off the cable TV in our house!

I know it may seem drastic, but my husband just said to me the other day, "You know, I don't miss it like I thought I would." Getting rid of the "time-suckers" will allow you to spend more time on the important things in life.

Use time as efficiently as possible. There are some things in your life that have to be done, but they don't take your full concentration. Use that to your advantage! For instance, many books are available on CD, or you can download them and put them on your iPod.

I like to listen to self-improvement or training materials while I am cleaning or driving. Need to return phone calls? Maybe you can use time during soccer practice to make calls while you're waiting in your car.

Plan your business tasks around your family's schedule. If you're like me, family is your top priority. I have set times for working on my business, when it does not conflict with time my family needs me. Don't be a slave to your business. Let people know when you are available, and people will know when they can call or expect a return e-mail from you.

Have a dedicated work space. If you have your business spread across the entire house, you will waste a lot of time looking for things that are in another place. Maybe you thought you left a document on the kitchen table, but it is actually in your bedroom.

If you have a dedicated work space, you will be more productive when you are working, and work is less likely to encroach on other parts of your life.

Chapter 5

Winning Strategy for Using Social Media to Grow Your Wealth

Using social media to market your business is a tricky journey. With so many options and so many wrong ways to do it, many business owners spend lots and lots of time (and money) trying to figure out this whole new world of building customer relationships and loyalty.

Many times all of the time and energy barely pays off with a splash of difference. It's time to get focused. Here is your winning social media marketing strategy for your business - any business, in fact.

First, you need to determine which web sites are right for your business. Some businesses may utilize one or two options, while others may benefit from many more. You don't necessarily need to know a lot about each site, but rather what people use each site for.

Users of Facebook, Twitter, Reddit, Linked-In, YouTube and the others spend time at the sites for different reasons. It's vital that you do research on why people use these sites and then if it makes sense to spend time marketing your business there.

Then you need to go on a field trip, with the purpose of watching and observing (not yet participating). The good news is that your field trip will cost you no money, but rather an investment of your time. And it can be done from home, in your pajamas. All of your options are available 24 hours a day, 7 days a week, 365 days a year.

Since most business owners and managers have little time during business hours to spend on social media marketing, much can be done at other times. Your field trip will consist of going to the sites that you're considering using for your business and observe how the people engage and communicate with one another.

Don't participate just yet, but rather just observe how more veteran users are behaving (posting, tweeting, submitting, updating).

Next, and this is a very, very important part of your strategy, is to understand the difference between "push" marketing and "pull" marketing. Once you decide to take your business online, you must treat your customers and potential customers with the highest respect and consideration.

Your marketing efforts online will not be successful if you plan to just promote your business or your product in "old-school" marketing ways like couponing, discounts and specials ("push" marketing).

You'll get much more positive results if you use social media to build long term relationships with your customers, to build their trust, and to provide them with a unique and cutting edge way of communicating with you ("pull" marketing).

Now, you need to learn the facts. Lots of data is available on the habits of social media users. Sure, there are hundreds of millions of users. But when is the best time to communicate with your target customers and how?

Are some days better than others to post and tweet? Can you post and tweet too little or too much? Should you use just text or pictures and videos, as well? Getting answers to these questions and more will save you lots of time and energy, and increase your chances of having a successful strategy.

Finally, it's time to dive in, but do so smartly. When registering for social media sites, be mindful of the branding of your business.

Go to the help section of the sites to find out what's available for businesses (for instance, at Facebook and Google+, there are personal profiles and business profiles, but at Twitter and Linked-In, that's not the case).

Make sure your social media "footprint" is in concert with the spirit and integrity of your brand, including your logo, tag line, colors, texture and tone. Be courteous, inviting and accessible.

Don't look to sell your product or service to people (the "push"), but rather provide them with tips and information about your product and service (the "pull"). And be ready to interact with people, hopefully responding to questions and requests for information quickly and efficiently.

Chapter 6

What Marketing Strategy is the Best for You to Grow Your Wealth?

If you pick the right marketing strategy, you'll be like that little guy in the middle of my diagram above. Yes! Winning! Fist pumps!

The problem with marketing today is that there are way too many options and it's much too confusing. It makes me dizzy just thinking about this stuff and I've been immersed in it for 35 years.

Well, I lay down on my bed last week with a notepad and started to map out my "Unified Theory of Marketing Strategies" with an emphasis on online marketing.

And I actually came up with something that's not totally confusing, and might even be helpful to a few people.

It's yet another four-quadrant grid where the vertical axis is a scale from easy to hard and the horizontal axis is a scale from passive to proactive.

I emerged with these four snappy quadrants:

Hard and Passive = Multimedia
Easy and Passive = Publishing
Hard and Proactive = Presentations
Easy and Proactive = Email

Now, all of these strategies can be effective. But, yes some are easier than others. And the passive ones tend to take a lot longer than the proactive ones.

Hard and Passive = Multimedia (Videos)

Everyone is crazy about video these days. It's a challenging, yet passive strategy. You put a lot work into creating a video and then post it on YouTube hoping people see it.

It's difficult to do well. It's time-consuming and it can be expensive. And most videos are pure crap. If you want to do it well, it takes a chunk of change and a lot of time.

Throwing up a lot of little videos on your website can be a nice touch, but they usually don't get people to call you in droves.

So, as you can see, I'm not crazy about a video strategy for self-employed professionals. I'm not saying they can't work, but it's a whole lot of work to do right.

Easy and Passive = Publishing

I happen to like this strategy a lot as it, ahem, built my "Empire." It's relatively easy: Write a how-to article on your subject matter once a week, send it out to those on your e-list and publish on your blog. Fame ensues.

But online publishing can be a lot more than that. You can take those same articles and publish them on Medium, LinkedIn, and Ezine Articles. And then you can announce them on Facebook, Twitter, Instagram, and Pinterest. Sometimes you can get big exposure when writing an article for a major online publication. Web traffic multiplies.

The cost is zero; an article takes from two to five hours to write (unless it takes you several days). And your ideas are online for eternity to be discovered by those looking for practical ideas. Some will opt-in to your e-list and perpetuate this virtuous marketing circle.

The downside, of course, is that, according to my extensive research, (a 10 second Google search), there are 2 million articles published online every day. The mind reels. So your stuff will be out there, but somewhat lost in a very big haystack.

I'm still a big advocate of online publishing, but the mountain is getting steeper and steeper. Just writing an article or two here and there won't help you much.

Best Example: Well, other than mine, of course, check out Henneke of Enchanted Marketing. She has a wonderful, readable, fun blog on business writing and blogging. And she walks her talk. It's all about well-written, relevant content. If you don't have that as a foundation, it's a total waste of time.

Hard and Proactive = Presentations

I built my business on presentations in front of live audiences at professional associations and chambers of commerce. It got me attention, added people to my mailing list and generated warm leads for marketing coaching.

And I still do presentations today in the form of webinars. I just filled my recent group program with the help of a couple webinars (also called video conferences). They most certainly do work.

But I put presentations in the hard category, not because they are all that hard to give, but can take a long time to prepare. The last one I did took me two full days. There were about 200 slides (whew).

Yes, that's not the only way to do a webinar. You can just go live on Zoom Video, and that can work as well. You ultimately have to find your style and test what works.

Presentations are proactive in that at the end you can ask for the business. And, of course, you can turn the recording of the webinar into a video in a snap and send it out to those on your list. Watch it here.

So presentations will always play a big part in my marketing toolkit.

One other thing though - If you don't have a LOT of people on your email list, good luck in getting much of an attendance. Yes, you can do guest presentations hosted by others, but you don't have the same control and ability to pitch your professional services.

Best example: John Nemo of LinkedIn Riches (linkedinriches.com). His webinar is a blast. There are a lot of them out there in the online marketing world. And many, Like John, have set them up as evergreen webinars that are scheduled to play automatically several times a day. These are kind of a hybrid between publishing and presentations.

Easy and Proactive = Email

In my opinion, email is the most powerful overall marketing tool. And it gets the least respect. But I can't imagine even being in business without email marketing.

Social media gets all the PR and all the attention, but email gets the business. A recent study showed that email generated 40 times the business results of Facebook and Twitter combined.

Email is the online tool that's been around the longest, and I think it's taken for granted. Promotional emails have expanded exponentially over the years, but most of it isn't very good.

We wade through our email boxes like we sort our mail over the trashcan. Delete, delete, delete. Why? Because it's either not relevant or it's boring. Usually both.

I feel that email has the greatest potential of all the online marketing strategies because it's both relatively easy and the most proactive marketing medium of all. Your message goes right into the mailbox of your potential client. Nothing else can do that.

Marketing email holds great opportunities for improvement in several areas:

1. How to incorporate humor as the most powerful attention-getting device in existence (that almost nobody is using).

2. How to telegraph your value proposition straight to the minds and hearts of your prospect.

3. How to make your emails clear, focused, and easy-to-read.

4. How to craft a compelling call-to-action that is hard to resist.

5. How to get emails to thousands of your prospects without looking like spam.

If you're not working on ALL of these, your emails will not get the attention and response you want.

Best Example: Therapy Practice Accelerator. Visit this site and get on the list just to see the brilliance of the email marketing. It's all about demonstrating results.

What marketing strategies will you choose?

Take the four marketing quadrants into consideration. The easier a marketing activity, the more likely you'll actually do it. And the more proactive a marketing activity, the faster the response you'll get.

Chapter 7

Financial Asset Management - Manage Your Wealth

Financial asset management, or wealth management as it is sometimes called, is the management of your financial assets. Many people know how to make money, but they are clueless when it comes to managing the money that they make in order to secure their financial future, or to reach financial goals that they have set.

Management of your finances and your assets is not something that is limited to big corporations or even to businesses; in fact, many individuals can benefit from the advice of a financial manager.

What Do Financial Asset Managers Do?

A financial asset manager is a person that works with individuals or companies to meet the goals that they have set by properly managing the financial resources that they. Goals may include buying a first home or another home, saving for their children's education, planning for retirement, or accumulation of wealth.

The Planning Process

Financial managers will work with their clients through a planning process that will allow the goals that they have set for their financial future to come to fruition. This may include analysis of the person or business' income, taxes, expenses, current retirement plans, insurance coverage, trusts, wills, and more.

This gives the financial asset manager an idea of the person or business' overall financial situation so that strategies and objectives can be identified and then developed to achieve the goals that you have.

The financial asset management process can include the following services: cash flow analysis, planning for taxes, retirement and education, estate recommendations, investments and review of your insurance to make sure that you and your family are covered completely with the types of policies that you need to protect your assets in the event of sickness or death.

Investments

A big part of financial asset management usually involves investments. A financial manager can help to identify the investments that can make your wealth grow, including stocks, bonds, index funds, mutual funds, and other securities that are publicly traded.

Many people are a bit gun-shy in today's economic environment when it comes to investing, so a good financial manager can help you find well-researched investment strategies to manage your wealth in a way that can secure the future that you have always envisioned and make the most use of the money that you have right now.

Choose your financial manager wisely, and make sure that they are fully trained (usually with an MBA certification) so that you can feel more secure in giving them access to your funds.

6 Questions to Test Your Wealth Building Strategies

If you want to test out your own financial habits against some recommended wealth building strategies, the answers may help you to start to build wealth in your lifetime. How is it possible that an ordinary couple on ordinary income built extraordinary wealth becoming multi-millionaires and retiring in their fifties?

This is the premise of the Automatic Millionaire by David Bach, one of 12 best-selling books in personal finance. The strategy he presents is not as far-fetched as the story appears.

Instead of focusing on growing your income, increasing your spending and looking rich, if you switch to saving money, investing wisely, you can become very rich - and sooner than you might think. It's simple to read, but it seems difficult for people to implement in today's increasingly materialism and credit-orientated culture.

As a regular on the Oprah Winfrey show, David Bach is no stranger to the personal finance industry, at least in the US. But what sets him apart from many experts are the straightforward strategies he shows, which anyone can do to become debt free and build wealth in your lifetime.

Here are six questions you can ask yourself to kick off your own personal wealth building strategies and finish rich in your lifetime.

1. Do You Want to be Rich?

This is not a trick question. But the real question is to ask yourself WHY you want to be rich.

If you get clear on your goals, you wake up hungry to make it happen and you're more likely to do the work and make the sacrifices to achieve them.

2. Do You Pay Yourself First?

This is the number one financial decision, but few of us do it and certainly we don't do it automatically. When you earn a dollar, the first person who should get paid is YOU. Pay yourself first means put money aside for your taxes, your retirement accounts, your savings, many of which are tax free!

The rule is to pay yourself one hour a day of your income - around 10-15% - invested automatically for life. (The average household actually puts away only 10 minutes worth of their earnings a day - around 2% - which is both shocking and scary.)

3. Do You Know Your Latte Factor?

The average American and probably European spends around $10 a day on incidental purchases, like buying a Latte and a pastry before, during and/or after work, maybe a pack of sandwiches or a salad and a drink over lunchtime. If it's not that, it's a magazine or an extra CD, grabbing some chocolate at the petrol station.

That $10 a day amounts to $3600/year (assuming that somehow you will have a latte factor not just on weekdays but weekends too). If you put that away instead, it really mounts up - and this will blow your mind.

Calculate it through at say 8% annual growth, over 35 years, that is actually a staggering $1,385,505 - over a million dollars - for coffee! Wait five more years, and that would be an unbelievable $2,108,569.

The strategy here is to become conscious of what your incidental 'latte' purchases are and reduce them or knock them out and instead pay yourself first with it.

4. Do You Rent or Own?

If paying yourself first is the number one financial decision, then the number one investment decision is buying your own home. It's the top wealth creation strategy you can use. Home owners have a net worth of 40-50 times more than people who rent.

A secondary strategy is to pay your mortgage debt off as early by making over payments and thus saving enormous amounts of money on interest otherwise paid. But a third arm to this is that once you've paid about half off, use the equity to buy another property of the same value an rent it out.

For a 15 year long fixed rate mortgage, the interest rates are as low as they will probably ever be and it is easier than ever to benefit and build wealth in your lifetime. In fact, using a bi-weekly payment plan could save you over six figures in interest over 15 years!

5. Do You Have Debt?

If you are going to work really hard to make money, then you should make sure you have a plan to keep it! The only economy you can control is your personal economy, so reduce your debt by paying it off from the start and little by little. This is easier and less stressful than trying to pay off big lump sums.

6. Do You Give Back?

When your personal finances are stretched, it seems very hard to consider any level of tithing. But it's a healthy habit and pays you back in so many ways. It's another kind of wealth. When you feel happiness and satisfaction at a deeper level, you are far more open to opportunities you might otherwise never notice.

Why is Wealth Management Important?

No matter what age you are, Wealth Management is extremely important. Although most people don't bother to learn about wealth management until later in their life, it is a vital skill that should be taken into consideration by any individual that has accumulated some form of wealth.

This chapter will describe why wealth management is important, and will offer some ideas on different places that you can invest your money confidently as a part of your own personal wealth management strategy.

Wealth management is the process of investing your wealth and planning out a strategy so that your money "works" for you, ensuring that you will continue to be comfortable financially throughout your lifetime.

Wealth management does not only imply that you are focused on saving money in the present; it also means taking that money and investing it into financial vehicles to make even more money (aka having your money "work" for you).

People who practice a proper wealth management strategy will fair better financially throughout the course of their lifetime in comparison to individuals who do not follow a strategy.

If you're entirely new to investing, it is best to consult with a financial advisor that can help you in planning your wealth management strategy. Don't ever invest your money blindly; it is important that you know how to invest, how much to invest, and when to invest.

If you are ready to start your own wealth management strategy and have money to invest, you are probably wondering where you should invest your money. Here are two good places to invest your money that many smart investors are cashing in on in today's financial markets:

1. Canadian Stock Market – Investors love to get involved in the stock market because they can use their own personal knowledge to help give them an edge in predicting smart investments.

With the stock market, there is a diverse array of stocks that investors are able to choose from. Because Canada has maintained a stable business environment, the Canadian stock market is especially attractive to investors.

2. Mining Stocks – There are all sorts of mining stocks that investors are currently investing in. From gold and silver stocks, to uranium and even coal stocks, investors seeking an attractive return without too much risk are increasingly buying into a variety of mining stocks.

Wealth management is a skill that should be learned and practiced from the moment an individual begins to generate a healthy income. It involves much patience, skill, and financial knowledge, to know how to make your money grow, and it is also important to have an understanding of which investments are wisest for you invest in before entering into your own wealth management strategy.

Chapter 8

Avoiding Financial Disaster in Wealth Building

Creating wealth is as dangerous as stalking a wild animal: if we do not understand everything possible about money and treat it with respect and manage it with great skill it will destroy us as quickly as any beast of prey.

Return of the Warriors

According to Theun Mares in his book The Return of the Warriors "life is as much about hunting today as it was in the past when men were the hunters going out each day to hunt for food". In those days they took the hunt very seriously.

Hunting animals was a dangerous business and if you put a foot wrong you could end up being the food rather than bringing it home. On the other hand if you simply sat at home and waited for the food to appear it very rarely did.

Hunting Money Requires Total Dedication

Today we no longer have to hunt for food; we buy it at the supermarket with money. But don't kid yourself nothing has changed. While we no longer hunt for food we still have to hunt for the money with which we buy it.

Sitting at home waiting for the money to arrive is about as stupid as the hunter waiting for the Kudu to politely arrive at the door and accidentally fall into his cooking pot. We have to go out and stalk it.

The hunter leads a disciplined life and is totally dedicated to hunting. The hunter is a disciple of hunting and directs all his efforts towards knowing everything possible about hunting. And stalking money is as dangerous as stalking a wild animal.

Money Has No Mercy

Creating wealth is exactly the same: if we do not understand everything possible about money and treat it with respect and manage it with great skill it will destroy us as quickly as any beast of prey.

Money is a slave and it works for whoever puts it to work. Money will provide the best return to those who manage it correctly and will destroy those who show it little respect. Money has no mercy.

In the same way that a hunter lives the hunt to the full in order to succeed, so we today must direct our full attention towards money if we wish to conquer it and succeed in this arena of wealth creation. Wealth does not fall into anyone's hands by chance; it has to be captured with patience, slowly and carefully.

Generating Wealth

A wealth generation plan or budget is one in which:

You hunt money with dedication, integrity and care.

Your target is to get every rand of income to generate another rand. This is the ideal and you may never quite achieve it; but the closer you get the wealthier you will be.

Wealth generation and financial security come first; you come second and luxuries come last.

Your first target is to stop paying PAYE Tax; in other words to eventually earn an income other than from a job.

Your second target is to put seed capital before any other outflow or expense; that is to allocate the very first part of your (after tax) income to investing money in such a way that it will bring back more money - i.e. growing your money. The secret of wealth is acquiring income generating assets.

Your third target is to set aside money to get out of debt.

Your fourth target is money to meet your monthly financial security goals.

What is left will have to meet the balance of your needs and keep you alive and healthy - e.g. food, clothing etc.

Wealth Protection Checklist

If we combine wealth-protection, wreck-proofing and Kiyosaki's three stages of wealth-creation we end up with a 3 stage wealth-protection checklist that will work something like this depending on your needs and circumstances:

Stage 1 – Financial Security Involves:

Setting out your investment philosophy and your investment guidelines which incorporate your lifestyle and financial priorities. "Warren Buffett Wealth" by Robert P. Miles is an excellent guide.

Writing down the broad outline of a wealth creation and wealth protection plan (that is divorce friendly!)

The introduction of a wealth creation budget with seed capital

Having correctly structured books of account and financial statements for both personal affairs and businesses - regard yourself as "JB Smith Ltd" and monitor your WC budget and NAV monthly and annually with a simple accounting package

Banking right - maintaining a good bank credit rating

Maintaining a good credit rating with retail stores

Ensuring correctly structured tax returns and business activities that minimise taxes and maintaining a good standing with the local Revenue Service

Maintaining a healthy lifestyle and hospital protection as opposed to expensive medical aid

Disability insurance (tax deductible in certain countries)

Cost effective life insurance for the longest possible term with future protection (guaranteed future option on life cover)

Funeral cover

A correctly formulated will

Motor vehicle, household and all risk insurance

Your personal motor-car-maintenance plan to hold the asset value as high as one can

You personal household-maintenance plan to hold the asset value as high as one can

Working hard in a job and on your wealth protection strategy

Being a passive investor - still strongly dependent on the guidance of financial experts. A risk management Strategy with emphasis on moderate-risk and long-term investments

A personal book-of-life that holds all your insurances, life policies, RAs, assets and liabilities, SOGW worksheet and will in one place

A wealth plan work sheet with a list of assets and liabilities, purchase costs, improvement costs, dates of acquisition etc.

A financial literacy programme and

"The Science of Generating Wealth" by Wallace D Wattles

Stage 2 - Financial Comfort Involves:

Retirement planning and tax deferred retirement investing that provides maximum tax free income on retiring

Estate and tax optimization plan

Educational plan for the kids

Running your own business on the side

Establishing a mastermind advisory panel which includes an ontological leader coach

Paying for your car in 3 years and holding it for 6; i.e. paying off two cars in 6 years

Paying your bond in 10 years or less, accessing the bond for cheap finance (especially for motor car and credit card debt), and ensuring via a bond broker that you always have the lowest bond rate

Buying pre-owned time share

Tax efficient investment plans such as endowments

Endowment based holiday plan to fund quarterly breaks annual holidays and overseas travel

Dread disease insurance

Inter-vivos and business trusts to protect assets where cost effective

Medical aid appropriate to your health condition and family needs

Life cover and retirement investments for spouse

Optimization of wealth creation budget - maximizing the percentage of money working for you

Optimization of NAV growth

Strict cash flow management

Risk management strategy with emphasis on moderate risk investments and risk containment

Collective investments (unit trusts/mutual funds) and other moderate risk long-term investments - 10 years or more

Emergency fund - 3 months income in low risk liquid investments

Work hard and smart

More active investor - taking charge and responsibility for your wealth - less dependent on the decisions of financial experts

Wealth protection and wealth creation in balance

Financial literacy programme continues

Experience stage of financial literacy programme - learning from mistakes

Stage 3 - Wealth and Excessive Cash Involves:

Active and independent investor - all your money working for you one way or another and achieving your desired ROI

Resigned from your job to mange your wealth plan full time

Business optimization: business works without you and achieves desired ROI

Business succession plan in place

Buying value business investments or acquiring assets without money

Business investments and acquisitions continue to flourish

Acquiring portfolio investments - share market investments

Refined risk management strategy with a mix of more aggressive investments

Diversification of risk including 20-30% offshore investments

Property investments generating recurring income

Working smart and loving what you do every minute of the day

Living in your ideal home and driving a cost efficient luxury car

No problem you can't handle

Active independent investor and business owner - calls on experts for their expert opinion but makes own decisions

Low maintenance recurring and passive income

Sustainable creation of excessive cash a daily habit

Continuing to learn from active involvement but now with fewer mistakes

No Need to Retire

When it comes down to real wealth there are no shortcuts. Creating real wealth takes time. It is a marathon. It takes 15 to 30 years and it initially involves work. So the sooner you begin the better. But the good news is that when you are wealthy you never retire and you never work.

Hard work however is all relative. If you do what you love work is never hard. Warren Buffett at the age of 76 says that he "Tap dances to work" each day. He has a wealth protection based approach to investing that reduces risk to a minimum and optimises income and his system has made him either the first or second wealthiest person in the world.

The rich put immediate comfort and luxuries before wealth. They laugh first for sure, but it does not last, and when it really matters they are crying while the wealthy are having the last laugh.

But those who laugh last laugh longest and with this plan when you get round to laughing you will laugh long and hard because you have your priorities in the right order.

Chapter 9

The Most Important Rule of Investing to Build Your Wealth

A friend of mine recently bought a $30 stock that suddenly fell to $20. He invested quite a bit into this stock - so now he's having trouble sleeping. He wants to 'ride it out' until his stock returns to $30, but in the meantime, he's sick over this!

When he told me about it, I realized that his main trading focus in on finding an undervalued company that's about to soar! If he can find such a company, he'll make a killing! His emphasis is on MAKING money. But that's why most individual traders generally do poorly in the stock market.

Most successful investors would agree that the #1 most important rule of investing is:

"Don't Lose Money."

It's critically important to understand that in order to recoup a loss, a stock will need to achieve a higher percentage gain than it lost. Huh?

Let's go over a simple example to clarify what I'm talking about.

Let's say I bought a stock for $30 a share and it lost 33% of its value by falling to $20. BUT, when that $20 stock achieves a 33% gain, its price will be at only $26.60 - not $30 yet.

In order for that $20 stock to return to its previous price of $30, it will need to achieve a 50% gain! A 33% loss requires a 50% gain to break even.

How often does ANY stock quickly increase in value by 50%? Not often.

A 50% loss in value requires a 100% gain to break even. Its value needs to DOUBLE! You can grow old waiting for that to happen!

Therefore, the #1 rule of investing is not about making money, it's about cutting your losses short. Big losses are very difficult to recoup. We all know people who lost a huge chunk of their retirement accounts due to our crazy market. If they were focused on the rule "Don't lose money", they'd still have their nest eggs intact.

Always implement a simple strategy called a "stop-loss." A "stop-loss" is a trading feature that will sell your stock automatically and immediately if the stock value falls below a certain price.

It "stops your losses." If you buy a $30 stock, you might set a "stop-loss" point of $27.50 so that if the stock suddenly falls in price, it will automatically sell your shares on the way down. In our example of a $30 stock that fell to $20, you would have sold at $27.50 and avoided a 33% loss - if you had implemented a "stop-loss" value.

You can also use the "stop-loss" feature to lock in profits. For example, let's say you purchase a stock for $30 and set the "stop-loss" point at $27. But as you hoped, the stock price goes up to $35.

That's the time to move your "stop-loss" price up to $34. This way if the value drops back to $30, you will have automatically sold at $34 - which locked in a 13% gain.

The basic idea is to invest conservatively, limit your losses, and lock in your gains.

Chapter 10

The Fundamental Secret of Wealth

1. The truth is that riches (I mean real wealth) come from doing business yourself and not from earning wages, salaries or fees.

2. Speculate. Think deeply, discuss, invest and believe strongly in something not entirely certain.

3. The SWOT analysis: Strength, Weaknesses, Opportunities and Threats must be mastered.

4. Take action. According to an old Senegalese proverb "The opportunities that God sends to us do not wake up those who are asleep". This is because sleep is for the lazy, indolent and the poor. While wide awake is for the hungry, the lean, the opportunity taker and the rich.

5. The longer you take to make your money, the more diverse you will be with your investments and income streams. Make your money slowly and you will enjoy your money more. It will last longer and you will sleep properly at night.

Easy Rules of Wealth

1. Do not leave your money idle: either at home or in an inactive bank account. Plunge it into profitable investments or move it into around to high interest accounts, even if it is for a short period.

2. There could be a better interest rate for you somewhere else, always be on the lookout and search for it. Never be satisfied with the interest rate are receiving now even if it is high.

3. Do not continue to wait for the proper time, so as not to lose the right opportunity, do what you have to now. The more you take your time the more money you waste. Time is money and any money kept idle is wasted money.

4. Before investing in anything of value, make sure that it is useful and it will appreciate in value.

5. Never leave your properties empty. It may be increasing in value and you are missing valuable rental income.

6. Shop around for goods and services you are paying for. There may be cheaper options out there. Do not just pay for a name, pay for quality.

7. Never be satisfied with your achievements, always be prepared to for ways to improve, enhance, and develop yourself for progress in your endeavors. Explore all available options.

Chapter 11

Wealth Management and Wealth Attraction

When talking about possession, a person unconsciously refers to wealth. But depending upon its use, wealth can be defined in different ways. Basically, it can be classified into financial and non-financial.

Financial Wealth In the economic world, wealth is defined owning items which have economic values. Example of having financial wealth is the accumulation of things like real estate, money and jewelries.

When talking about possession, a person unconsciously refers to wealth. But depending upon its use, wealth can be defined in different ways. Basically, it can be classified into financial and non-financial.

Financial Wealth

In the economic world, wealth is defined owning items which have economic values. Example of having financial wealth is the accumulation of things like real estate, money and jewelries. There are reasons why people try to have financial wealth. The most common reason is security.

People with financial wealth also believe that having them brings power, respect and recognition. Depending on where you live, the amount of financial wealth you have accumulated will be relative.

Wealthy individuals living in third world countries would be considered average in countries like the United Kingdom and United States.

Non-financial Wealth

While other people are occupied with the accumulation of material wealth, other people believe that true wealth is not something that has economic value. Faith, love and peace of mind are just some of the examples of non-financial wealth that some people strive hard to have in their life. The reasoning behind is simple. Even with all the material wealth in the world, a person would never feel truly complete or secured without non-financial wealth.

In recent years, society has finally looked at non-financial wealth as equally important as financial wealth. Ironically, some people need to spend money just to obtain non-financial wealth.

They enroll in yoga or meditation classes to have peace of mind, donate huge amounts of money to participate in religious activities and even buy their loved ones expensive gifts to show their love and appreciation.

It is therefore obvious that people have integrated these two types of wealth to define the true meaning of the word. To achieve or create financial and non-financial wealth, here are some of the most common practices.

To achieve financial wealth, you can harvest natural resources and/or develop or change a material thing thru skills and knowledge application. Another way to create wealth is by improving methods in production, effectively creating wealth faster.

You can decide to set a limit to your accumulation of financial wealth depending on your need for security. On the other hand, non-financial wealth can be achieved or created by analyzing your needs and priorities.

You can only achieve peace of mind if you know what you want in life. Since non-financial wealth is not quantifiableFeature Articles, it is difficult to realize whether or not you have enough of it in your life.

Chapter 12

Applying SWOT (Strengths, Weaknesses, Opportunities, and Threats) Analysis to Growing Wealth

In order for any business owner to fully understand their business they need to periodically perform a SWOT analysis. Simply put, SWOT is a complete evaluation of the owner of a business, all of the employees, and all of the business resources.

A SWOT analysis pinpoints every activity and then identifies what is done well, where and in what areas need to be improved upon, and whether or not you take advantage of all the opportunities that are presented to the business.

A SWOT analysis shows every area where changes need to be made in order to make the most of those business opportunities the company is presented with.

Performing a SWOT analysis is critical because it can show the internal strengths and weaknesses of the owner of the business, all of the employees, the business itself, and the products and or services that are being offered. At the same time it will also show you what opportunities are available.

Here are a few examples; have there been any changes in the market that could ultimately affect your business? What about changes with the way people are buying your products or using your service? Are there any financial issues that are of special concern to you now or possibly down the road?

Now that you have an idea of what a SWOT analysis is, this is the best way to go about doing one.

Take several sheets of paper and at the very top label each one appropriately. STRENGTHS, WEAKNESSES, OPPORTUNITIES, THREATS. Make sure that you take your time with this; it can be a long process when you start thinking about everything.

Also, try to be as objective as possible, maybe ask for input from other individuals that are also versed with information on your company business, personnel, and financial situation.

STRENGTHS. Look at your business and evaluate what it is that you do well. How do you treat your customers? Do you make them feel comfortable and welcomed in your store or office? Do you display a grateful attitude that they chose your store over the competition?

What do you do to support customer loyalty? How do you market your business? How would you describe the location of your store? Is it easily accessible? Is there enough parking? Is everything jammed into a small space making it difficult to see all that you offer?

How knowledgeable is your staff? Are they always courteous, do they go out of their way to make your customers feel special? For instance do you offer any incentives to your employees for going above and beyond in helping customers to gain loyalty, referrals and more? List everything positive under the strength column.

WEAKNESSES. After careful consideration recognize all of your weaknesses. What are you and others currently doing that you feel you could improve upon? Are you late with any of your orders or shipping your products?

Do you have enough capital to purchase the products you need or just enough money to purchase exactly what you need? Do your suppliers deliver your products on time so that you can complete your orders? Do you have enough sales help so that you are not keeping your customers waiting?

You may want to change places and become a customer when doing this exercise. Being as objective as possible, how would you rate your business? Would you be happy with the service that you have been given and want to continue doing business, or have you had problems that have not been properly taken care of by the customer service department?

Do you hear excuses when complaints are made? Does the sales staff attempt to disregard any suggestions customers may make? Is the sales staff happy and upbeat, and is that conveyed to the customers?

OPPORTUNITIES. Look at all of your opportunities. Changes in the marketplace and consumer buying habits provide a wealth of information, giving you the opportunity to take advantage of situations long before someone else in the same industry.

Are you the only business within 100 miles or so thereby creating a captive audience? You may have some of the same factors here and in the strength category. How do you differ from your competition? How is your sales staff in comparison to the competition? Do they display a friendlier attitude?

Does your business offer the same services or can you offer a wider variety? Would you have added opportunities if you increased the size of your sales staff? Would you have additional opportunities if you hired a manager with more experience than the current manager?

Would you have increased profits if you had additional capital for marketing? If you enlarged your space would it enable you to display more merchandise and increase your profits? If you had the opportunity to carry merchandise that complimented each other, would that increase your profits?

This category can really give you the chance to explore what you would like to do if you have the chance and the capital. So let your imagination get a little carried away.

THREATS. This category can be a little like deductive reasoning. Some threats are apparent and easily recognizable while others are not. In this category you could imagine if key employees quit, how would this impact your business?

One of your suppliers went out of business and was the only manufacturer of that particular product. You suddenly needed capital and did not have it and did not have any resources to get it.

A business just like yours just opened a few miles away. Your business had a fire and you had to relocate. Think about all of the worse case scenarios that could happen and the affect they would have on your business and write them all down. prepares you for the unexpected and put you into a position to act quickly to lessen the negative impact on your business.

After you have completed this exercise look at everything you have written down in each category. I can guarantee that you will see your company in a whole new light. You should have a better understanding of where you are currently and what needs to be amended to maximize your company's potential.

It will also show you how to turn all of the threats into opportunities. Using this type of strategy will show you how to evaluate your business and as previously mentioned should be done every so often as your business is constantly changing. It's like a road map for business success.

Having envisioned a worst case scenario, you are now prepared and able to implement positive changes that will help your business for years to come.

Chapter 13

The Dangers in Wealth Building

Many of my friends and colleagues have taken a serious hit since the financial and property market meltdown in 2008. Indeed, much of what people worked for all their lives has vanished as their asset values fell off a cliff.

Some have even lost their businesses and others are grappling with serious negative equity and massive debt attached to their real estate. But even as everyone wrestles with these financial challenges, they're finding new opportunities and these opportunities are not under their mattresses!

There is always opportunity in crisis. On a personal level this is a great time for re-assessing your life goals and values. From a wealth building perspective, apart from snapping up distressed assets at bargain-basement prices, possibly the true financial opportunity is something less obvious.

Perhaps it's the opportunity we have to realign our thinking regarding wealth and how we build it. Here's an outline of 4 steps you could take in order to start rebuilding your wealth.

Rebuilding Wealth Step #1: Reassess Your Portfolio

Chances are your investments are in totally different shape to where they were before the financial crisis. If you were an active investor, some of your stocks or real estate values may have taken a serious hit. At this point, it is your call whether to hope they will someday rebound or cut your losses.

If the yields are holding up on your real estate it may be worthwhile to 'trade out' of negative equity if positive cash-flow is still being generated. If any of your investments have produced capital gains, cashing in now could be a good idea and provide some capital for better investments. Re-assessing your portfolio is a great first step in rebuilding wealth.

Rebuilding Wealth Step #2: Rebalance Your Portfolio

Whether you were actively investing or more passively sitting on your assets, the financial crisis has probably taken your portfolio out of alignment. Balanced asset allocation is critical to long-term investment performance and wealth building.

Taking your risk tolerance and investment horizon into account will help work out what asset allocation works for you. Just because certain stocks might be performing well at the moment doesn't mean you should go chasing stocks and switch your cash out of bonds if bonds is where you need to be at right now.

Rebuilding Wealth Step #3: Rethink Your Wealth Building Strategy

In addition to seeking out high-performing assets, a fundamental rethink on how you build your wealth may be required. It may mean employing wealth building strategies that were put off during boom times.

Perhaps becoming financially literate should be a key objective right now. Rather than placing all your chips on high-performing stocks or property maybe you need to earn your right to invest and build up a solid foundation of cash or cash-equivalents (e.g. money market accounts, certificates of deposit etc) and bonds first.

It's recommended that at least 10% of your investment portfolio should be in cash or cash-equivalents at all times. This ensures you remain liquid so that a. You have funds to handle any financial circumstances ahead . You have funds to readily avail of possible investment opportunities.

I think that many of us were guilty of some fundamental wealth building blunder by being over invested in real estate and stocks without first having a solid base of cash, cash equivalents and bonds. Now is the time to re-adjust this imbalance.

Rebuilding Wealth Step #4: Focus on Growing Your Wealth

So, you're keeping winning investments or cash them in, weeding out the losers from your portfolio and realigning your asset allocation. What next? Well, now it's time to focus on increasing your returns and growing your investment portfolio. Whilst paying down debt, especially what I call 'bad debt', is hugely important, equally so is re-building your wealth with sound and advantageous use of 'good debt'. Focusing on building wealth is critical so that the focus isn't on debt reduction only.

Apart from hunting down real estate or other business opportunities in your state or country you really must think and act globally. You simply can't afford to rely on any one economy so don't be afraid to seek out opportunities in foreign territories and emerging markets.

Diversification by both asset type (stock, real estate, bonds etc) and geography has never been more appropriate.

So, rather than ever waiting for markets to change you can take charge of your own financial bailout and re-build your wealth. Re-assess and re-balance your portfolio. Rethink your wealth building strategy and then focus on growing your wealth.

Conclusion

The greatest investment you will ever make is an investment into your on-going personal development. No other investment will ever give you the same returns. As you consistently invest into your most important asset, namely your own self-development, the returns you will enjoy, go well beyond just gains in monetary wealth.

You become a better person in every respect. You are better equipped to be a better spouse, friend, employee, entrepreneur, etc. and if directed properly even your health will improve because health and wealth is closely associated.

Look at your life right now, are you investing at least 10 % of everything you earn each year, into your personal development?

If you are not and you are not satisfied with the results you are enjoying, then I highly recommend that you look to introduce this crucial growth strategy, where you commit to spend a minimum of 10 % of your annual income, on improving yourself, into your life today.

The level of success you get to enjoy is a mirror reflection of your self-identity and can never exceed your own self-development. Something this important deserves your full commitment and should be an integral part of your goals and planning for the future.

Your level of personal development is like the gauge on a thermostat. As you continue to improve, and grow, you gradually move your personal thermostat to a higher and higher number. As this number increases, so too does your personal set point or the limit of what you are capable of achieving.

A thermostat that is set at 22 degrees Celsius will regulate the temperature in a room and will introduce cold or heat as needed, to ensure the temperature in the room remains constant.

Your set point is exactly the same and is based on your level of personal development and the picture you have in your mind about your self-worth. No matter what happens in your environment, a financial windfall, and loss of weight on a strict diet or relationships seeming to go well, you will always return to your own set point, dictated by your level of personal development and self-worth.

Stop looking at the cost of your personal development and start to see the worth or value that it adds to your life. Any investment that you make into personal development materials, coaches or seminars is essentially free.

As you learn more, you eventually earn more and you become far more valuable than you would have remained, had you not invested into your personal growth. Look at your dreams and goals, does the investment you are making into your personal development match the size and scope of these goals and dreams?

When it does, you will catapult yourself forward and all your dreams and your financial fantasies will become reality.

My million dollar words of wisdom to you is that you concentrate on your personal development first before building your wealth.

From the Author's desk: Reviews are gold to authors! If you've enjoyed this book, would you consider rating it and reviewing it on Amazon.com?

www.ingramcontent.com/pod-product-compliance
Lightning Source LLC
Chambersburg PA
CBHW031923170526
45157CB00008B/3032